Prophetic Protocol
For Young Emerging Prophets

Madeline James

Copyright © 2018 Madeline James

All rights reserved.

ISBN-13: 978-1977752680

ISBN-10: 1977752683

DEDICATION

This book is dedicated to the emerging prophets in this hour. Be bold. Be fearless. Keep your heart pure and release the heart of the Father.

CONTENTS

Introduction   I

1 The Call   1

2 The Process   10

3 Realms of The Prophetic   22

4 Your Prophetic Voice   44

5 A Prophet's Lifestyle   55

6 Pitfalls   69

Endorsements

Madeline James has been anointed by God to sound the clarion call for this generation. She is an anointed Prophet that has accepted the call to shepherd a prophetic people in her thriving church plant.

In prophetic protocol you will grasp a deep theological understanding in to the mind of the Lord concerning prophets. You will be encouraged and challenged to interact in the spirit realm with honor and to respect the protocol of heaven. Madeline does a prolific job explaining the difference in the gift of prophecy, word of knowledge and word of wisdom. While not compromising on the message that Gods' people must be holy and that character has the power to grant or deny you access in the spirit.

This is a must-read book that should be added to the repertoire of prophetic schools and personal libraries.

Johnathan Stidham
Founder of Kingdom Global Network and Author

I believe that if you're looking for practical applications when it comes to the prophetic ministry, this is a great place to start!! Prophet Madeline has captured the heart of heaven as a prophet. From the beginning to the end, I was engaged! You can discern the voice of the Lord as she extends herself on prophetic protocol and etiquette. This is something that I feel is very much needed in the prophetic ministry today. From the call all the way to the pitfalls, she has nailed it. One of the things that stood out to me as a prophet was when she stated, the condition of your heart will affect your spiritual vision.

I believe that if you are ready to take your prophetic team and ministry to the next level, please make the prophetic investment and pre-order your copy today! Congrats prophet Madeline, one of our premiere emerging prophetic voices!

Deland John Coleman
Kingdom Church International and Author of Rising Of The Thoroughbreds

INTRODUCTION

In the last days, Joel 2 describes how the Lord will pour out His spirit upon all flesh and all would prophesy proclaiming the message of the Lord. The Lord is raising up a new remnant of young emerging prophets. These young prophets have not been mantled by men, but by the Lord. They're as multifaceted as Joseph's coat, and unique as David's red hair and freckles.

A prophet is marked from birth but proven through the process they're willing to submit to. The prophetic process is being accelerated and intensified, to produce prophets who won't flinch or shrink back in the face of adversity. Many prophets fail to last or burn out as fast as their rise, because they didn't allow the Father to fully process them.

Young prophet, to be seen and recognized in the earthly realm, you must be first recognized in the spirit realm. There is a standard and protocol to follow. Many resist the protocol, but it's meant to preserve you and guide you.

THE CALL

"NOW THE WORD OF THE LORD CAME TO ME SAYING, BEFORE I FORMED YOU IN THE WOMB I KNEW YOU, AND BEFORE YOU WERE BORN I CONSECRATED YOU; I HAVE APPOINTED YOU A PROPHET TO THE NATION." JEREMIAH 1:5

We are living in a time where many are being appointed prophets to the nations by the hand of man, instead of the hand of God. True prophets are handpicked by the Father from the foundations of the earth. Prophets are ==hardwired different== than those around them. ==They have built in faculties enabling them to be sensitive and receptive to hear and see the Word of the Lord==. Prophets tend to have peculiar personalities, process differently, and think outside the box. They are the square peg in a board made up of circle pegs. Most don't realize or become aware they're prophets till later in life. Being a prophet does not make one better, they just experience life through a different set of lenses.

Satan hates the prophetic and prophets because of their ability to create, speak life, and reveal the hidden things. The reality is, being a prophet puts a big bullseye on your back. If the enemy is unable to physically silence you, he'll try and kill your heart and emotions through the spirit of rejection.

Life in the Supernatural

Prophet, as you begin to step into your calling, you are going to be opened up to a new realm of the supernatural. As a prophet the supernatural will become as natural as breathing. Don't let the supernatural scare you or deter you. The supernatural will take some time to get used to and be calibrated to.

As a prophet you are called to govern the spirit realm over people, cities, regions, nations, etc. Because of that, it will become common to deal with different demonic spirits, powers, strongholds, and principalities (Ephesians 6). As you grow in your calling you'll learn how to work with the angels and how to function in the spirit realm with more ease. Throughout the Bible there are many examples of the prophets working with angels or receiving assistance from them.

It is important not to step out of your jurisdiction or realm of authority. Not all prophets have the same realm of influence or authority in the spirit realm. It's imperative to know your role as a prophet and stay in your lane to avoid unnecessary warfare. There is protocol in the spirit realm.

> *There is a protocol in the spirit realm.*

My Own Experience

From the time I was in my mother's womb the enemy tried to take my life. I was born with a hole in my heart. The first few months of my life were touch and go. I was hooked up to machines making sure I was breathing and that my heart didn't stop beating. Thankfully, my heart was able to heal on its own without any complications. Unfortunately, it wouldn't be the last time the enemy would make an attempt on my life.

Growing up I had a good childhood. My parents came from families that dealt with alcoholism and abuse, but with my brother and I they broke the generational curses of our family for us to walk in a new way. I remember being in church from the time I was little. I didn't know any different. I gave my heart to the Lord at age 5 in children's church. I'm very grateful to have grown up in the same church till I was 23 years old. It was a very healthy church that was led by the Spirit, and experienced continuous revival. I was able to grow up with men and women of God who poured into me from a young age, which set the spiritual foundation of my life.

> *Satan hates the prophetic and prophets because of their ability to create, speak life, and reveal. the hidden things.*

At a young age, I desired to function in ministry and tell people about Jesus. I would have dreams depicting these scenes. I remember coming back from a mission's trip upset I had to leave, because I was worried about who was going to tell the rest of the people about Jesus. My life was marked for the Lord.

I was a quiet and shy child. I didn't like being in big crowds, talking in front of others, or being in loud places, because it would overwhelm me. Although I may not have shown much emotion on the outside, like a true introvert there was always an emotional storm inside. In school I excelled in my studies and played sports. When it came to popularity I was in the middle. I was friends with the popular and the outcast.

One of the major vices the enemy tries to use in the life of a prophet is rejection and being misunderstood. It's something a prophet will have to learn how to deal with and heal from. Unfortunately, I was not shielded from rejection and bullying. When you are marked for the Lord, no matter what age you are the enemy will send hurt and rejection to debilitate you. I was made fun off because I was a "Jesus freak." I was bullied because of the way I looked, and even in seminary I was made a spectacle by a group of girls. It was like a scene from the movie Mean Girls.

As a young person I was very emotional internally, which I didn't know was part of my prophetic make up. I battled depression, anxiety, an eating disorder and suicidal thoughts. I know I was a hot mess. I didn't understand the call on my life or understand why the enemy kept wanting to take my life. I didn't really know what a prophet was except for the prophets of the Bible. I knew I had the gift of discernment and could discern the hearts of those around me. I could look into someone's eyes and know their whole story. I had dreams that would come to pass verbatim in front of my eyes. Somehow, I just knew things. I thought this was normal, and everyone else could do the same.

My whole life the Lord was training me as a prophet but I didn't know it until one day everything changed.

THE NIGHT EVERYTHING CHANGED

It's important to understand that one cannot appoint themselves as a prophet. A man cannot give you this calling, and because you may prophesy well does not mean you're a prophet. A part of the protocol of stepping into the prophetic office is a true prophet who is called will have an encounter with the Lord, who will call them as a prophet (Ephesians 4:11). After the call has been placed upon your life, others will begin to notice and affirm the calling. Lastly, church leadership will begin to recognize, affirm, train, and as they see fit install you as a prophet.

The night I had my encounter with the Lord, I was in a season of transition. I was getting ready to leave my career as a counseling therapist and pursue the call of God on my life. During that time my dream life was awakened. I was having many encounters, and I began to dream God's dream for my life.

One night, I remember sleeping in my bed and I was suddenly awoken to a half awaken state. I heard all this noise coming from downstairs as if there was a party going on.

Suddenly, I heard this voice clear as day, "Madeline, Madeline" At first, I thought it was my husband and answered, "What?" After no answer I yelled back, "I'm upstairs." Then again, I heard that voice again say, "Madeline, Madeline." I answered again louder so my husband could hear, but to no avail. Then one more time, I heard that voice cut through the silence and call my name again, "Madeline, Madeline." When I woke up the next morning, I realized I had an encounter with the Lord like the prophet Samuel did when the Lord called him (1 Samuel 3).

Soon after that encounter others around me began to recognize and call me a prophet. This was not something I embraced at first. I almost wanted to deny it, because I understood the weight that came with the title. It was not something I took lightly. I thought it ironic the Lord would call a girl who hated to speak in front of others a mouthpiece for him.

As I looked back over my life, it now made sense why certain situations happened and why I saw things a certain way. I had been marked like Jeremiah from my mother's womb. Prophet you have been marked and set aside for such a time as this. It's time to own your call, and step into the prophetic mantle on your life. Your whole life has been a process leading up to your emerging. In your emergence there's a process, embrace the refining. The Lord is raising up pure prophets in this hour. Will you answer the call?

> *In your emergence there's a process, embrace the refining.*

THE PROCESS

THEN JESUS WAS LED BY THE SPIRIT INTO THE WILDERNESS (MATTHEW 4:1)

Once a prophet has an encounter with the Lord, it initiates God's processing in their lives. Really a prophet's whole life is training for what's to come. We never graduate the need for being processed. Even Jesus had to go through a process. It will be hard, vigorous, and stretch you beyond measure.

When you say yes to being God's mouthpiece, you give up your life and rights for His service. You are no longer yours, you are His. The platform doesn't come after the encounter, it comes after the Lord processes you. When God calls you as a prophet He takes you to the hidden place to process you. Think of the process of a photograph being developed. If the photograph is exposed too soon, the image will not be fully developed. It will come out distorted. I heard Christian Caine once say, "God has to make sure the light in you is greater than the spotlight, so the spotlight doesn't kill you when it hits you." The process isn't meant to kill you, but to prepare you for what's to come.

God takes you through the purification process to purify the motives, heart, intentions, ambitions, spirit, mouth… all of who you are. To fully embrace the process, you must fully submit your heart. Any place in your heart that is not submitted to the Lord's leadership, will eventually cause you to stumble.

The process isn't just about growing in your gifting, it's growing your character. Many have big gifting and talent, but little character to hold it up. There is a weight that comes with the prophetic office one must be able to carry. The prophetic office is vigorous, because it requires all of who you are. To be a prophet you cannot be halfway in, it must be all the way. When you are halfway in, you leave the door open to divination.

> *The platform doesn't come after the encounter, it comes after the Lord processes you.*

The Process Equips You

The process is meant to build you to handle the weight of the call. Often times when the Lord would call His prophets, He would equip them to handle the adversity that comes. Many know the prophetic call is hard, but until you are fully immersed in it, you won't have a true understanding for it. Often the Lord will use your weak place as his place of strength or ministry through you.

Each prophet is called to a certain people group and nations. The Lord tailors your process to be effective for the people group you are called to. When the Lord anointed and called the prophet Isaiah, he had to have his lips purified. Isaiah 6:5 says, "Then I said, 'It's all over! I am doomed, for I am a sinful man. I have filthy lips, and I live among a people with filthy lips.'" For Isaiah to be effective the Lord had to process his weak place, because it had been defiled being among the people. The Lord had to set apart Isaiah to be a pure voice among the people.

When the Lord ordained Jeremiah, he struggled with being young and fearful. God told him not to be afraid because it would become a trap for him. The Lord told Jeremiah, "Don't be afraid or I will make you look foolish in front of them. For see today, I have made you strong like a fortified city that cannot be captured, like an iron pillar or a bronze wall" (Jeremiah 1:17-18). In order for Jeremiah to be effective, God had to equip him with boldness and strength because the people were very intimidating.

When the Lord was releasing and commissioning Ezekiel, the Lord had to harden the mind and heart of the prophet. Ezekiel 3:89 says, "But look I have made you as obstinate and hard hearted as they are. I have made your forehead as hard as the hardest rock! So don't be afraid of them or fear their angry looks, even though they are rebels." Ezekiel could not do the work of the Lord with a tender heart and sensitive conscious, he would've been eaten alive by the people.

As a prophet the Lord knows your strong places and your weak places. Don't just focus on strengthening the strong places of your life. The enemy will always try to find an open door to the weak places in you and will exploit them. No prophet is Superman or invisible to the warfare that comes with the mantle. Allow the process to work its way in you.

Processing Everything About You

What makes the prophetic office unique and more intense than some other callings is, the prophet must submit all of who they are to God. The prophet's life is a prophetic message they walk out among others. A prophet's life is demanding and rigorous because all of who the prophet is will be used by God. To be a pure prophetic voice the prophet must allow the Lord to purify every facet of their being and senses, because they are representation of the Father's heart.

Eyes

The eyes of the prophet are one of the most important areas or functions to guard. Prophets do not only see in the natural, but they see in the realm of the spirit. This can be done through visions, inner visons, dreams and trances. The eyes are a gateway into the realm of the spirit. A prophet must mindfully and consciously guard their eyes, because they are a gateway that gives access to imprint on their spirit. You want to make sure the right things are being imprinted.

A prophetic person must guard what they allow their eyes to see. In a day an age where everything is so visually stimulating and graphic, you must sensor what you allow your eyes to see, because it will taint the filter through which you see people and in the realm of the spirit.

Be careful what you watch through movies, video games, television, and other visual mediums. These visual avenues are releasing violence, murder, lust, sexuality explicit scenes and so forth. Unfortunately, we have become a society where we've become used to seeing these images so much that they do not convict our hearts anymore.

> *The condition of your heart will affect your spiritual vision.*

A prophetic person is someone who must be sensitive to the things of the spirit. When there is no conviction, it creates a veil over your eyes and you are unable to see clearly. Matthew 5:8 says, "What bliss you experience when your heart is pure! For then your eyes will open to see more and more of God" (TPT). To see more in the realm of the spirit, you must keep your eye gates clean. When we allow ungodly images and visuals to cross through our eye gates, the filter through which we see becomes contaminated. Seeing in the spirit is not only connected to what you see but the condition of your heart.

Heart

The heart of a prophet is the mainframe through which the prophet operates. If your heart is off, everything you do will be affected by the impurity or purity of your heart. Proverbs 4:23 says, "So above all, guard the affections of your heart, for they affect all that you are. Pay attention to the welfare of your innermost being, for from there flows the wellspring of life" (TPT).

The condition of your heart will affect your spiritual vision. The process is rigorous in testing heart motives, because God desires to use pure prophetic vessels. Prophets cannot afford to allow unforgiveness, bitterness, rejection, lust, greed, etc. to fill their hearts. It will taint the prophetic flow and skew spiritual sight and insight. When we allow hurts, emotional issues, and heart matters to build up, it's like black tar that coats our hearts. The less light (truth) or illumination (understanding) that penetrates our hearts, the less we see. His illumination allows us to see clearly in the Spirit. In Ephesians 1:18 Paul prays, "I pray the light of God will illuminate the eyes of your imagination, flooding you with light, until you experience the full revelation of the hope of His calling" (TPT). It's His illumination that brings greater revelation. If our hearts become contaminated with impure motives, hurts and resentments we cannot see into the spiritual realm properly. We have no business releasing prophetic words when our hearts are in this state.

Being a prophet will draw attention to you because of the words you release. You must love the secret place more than the spotlight. Most of what prophets do is behind the scenes. Before you stand before man, you must learn to stand before the Lord.

Don't seek to please man, seek to please the Lord. The Lord entrusts His prophets with secrets. Prophets never use this information to manipulate others or boast. The Lord will stop sharing His secrets with you when they are used with impure motives. God will test your motives until you get them right because He has to be able to trust you with His Bride.

Mouth

As a prophet and prophetic person, your mouth is one of the main instruments that will be used. A prophet is a mouthpiece or an oracle of God, as one who speaks on His behalf. Speaking on behalf of the Lord is not something to be taken lightly. Just as your heart is a vessel, your mouth is vessel used to prophesy and declare the word of the Lord.

As a prophetic voice you cannot talk one way behind closed doors, and then another way while ministering. God will not honor your words. In Ephesians 4, Paul tells us not to let any unwholesome talk to precede from our mouths. When our words are laced with profanity, perverseness, bitterness, revenge, insults, and so on, we release witchcraft. May the fear of the Lord rest upon your life, to caution and guide what you release. Influence doesn't give a prophetic voice the right to release and say anything with no regard. There is a standard one must keep. Ephesians 4:30 says, "The Holy Spirit of God has sealed you in Jesus Christ until you experience your full salvation. So never grieve the Spirit of God or take for granted his holy influence in your life" (TPT).

Your mouth is a powerful tool. In Genesis 1 we see how God spoke the heavens and the earth into existence. Because we are made in His image we speak with the same creative and prophetic ability as the Lord. We have the power and ability to speak life and death from our mouth.

Words are containers that can carry power to shift and create. As a prophet there is a greater authority that rests upon your words. It's important to note when you are speaking your opinion, and when you are speaking on behalf of the Lord. As you begin to grow in the prophetic mantle, those around you will begin to take note and weight of what you're saying. When you start out in the prophetic and prophesy there is a grace given to prophesy whatever comes, just as when a baby is learning to walk before they run. As you mature there is a smaller window of grace to release just anything because, the authority and weight in the words you use grows as you mature.

Your Senses

Just as we have senses in the natural, we have spiritual senses that we operate through. Often those who operate more in the seer realm have a harder time managing their emotions and senses when they are growing in managing this gift. Hebrews 5:14 says, "But solid food is for the mature, whose spiritual senses perceive heavenly matter." Think of your spiritual senses sight, smell, touch, taste, and hearing like antennas that pick up certain frequency.

One of the goals of the enemy is to overwhelm and overload a person's spiritual senses so they freak out and try to shut down that gift in their life. A part of the process and maturing is learning what to tune into and learning what to tune out. Often times the enemy will try to get a person to take on something in the atmosphere or from the person next to them. The process will help you mature your senses and be able to discern properly without being overwhelmed and shutting down the gifting.

Process

As a prophet and prophetic person, the process is not something you skip, it's a prerequisite for functioning in the office of prophet. The ones who don't submit to the processing can be at risk for stepping into error and opening the door to divination. The process keeps you humble, submitted, and a pure prophetic voice the Lord can use. Those who allow the Lord to circumcise and process their hearts are those who He can trust.

Realms of The Prophetic

IN HIS GRACE, GOD HAS GIVEN US DIFFERENT GIFTS FOR DOING CERTAIN THINGS WELL. IF GOD HAS GIVEN YOU THE ABILITY TO PROPHESY, SPEAK OUT WITH AS MUCH FAITH AS GOD HAS GIVEN YOU. IF YOUR GIFT IS SERVING OTHERS, SERVE THEM WELL. IF YOU ARE A TEACHER, TEACH WELL. ROMANS 12:6-7

The prophetic can be confusing sometimes, because many assume those who prophesy are automatically prophets. That is not the case. As the Body of Christ, we must realize we have many parts, we're not all called to function in one way. In 1 Corinthians 12 and 14 Paul talks to the Church of Corinth as the gifts of the Spirt the Lord have given to His Church. These gifts are given to the Body of Christ to be an expression of Him, and to help encourage and build up the church using the gifts of the spirit.

We are not all called to be prophets, but we are called to be a prophetic people. As a prophetic people we can all to a degree prophesy and walk in the gifts of the Spirit as he wills. The Holy Spirit is the gateway into the prophetic realm. When one is not filled with the Holy Spirit, they can easily tap into the realm of the spirit through divination. The word of God and the Holy Spirit should be the only source of, and the way of navigation through the realm of the Spirit. Jesus says in John 10 and 14, He is the gate, the way and the truth.

> *We are not all called to be prophets, but we are called to be a prophetic people.*

Paul tells the church he wishes we would all prophesy. A person who walks in prophetic gifting will have a tendency to walk in one or two of the prophetic giftings, while a prophet will function in all prophetic realms. The prophetic realms are prophecy, word of knowledge, word of wisdom, spirit of prophecy, discerning of spirits, dreams and visions, and office of prophet.

Gift of Prophecy

It's important to learn to discern those who have the gift of prophecy from those who walk in the office of prophet. Paul tells us in 1 Corinthians 14 he wishes we would all prophesy. Prophecy is not something just for the prophets, but for the Body of Christ at large. We have put too much pressure on prophets to be the only ones to prophesy. When one speaks prophecy, it encourages and strengthens the whole Body of Christ.

A gift is an ability or talent God has given someone. To grow and mature a gift, one must exercise and work it to enlarge their gift. Those who walk in the gift of prophecy, it's something that comes natural to them. Paul tells in Romans that we prophesy according to our measure of faith. If you want to prophesy more step out in faith more. Prophecy requires risk.

As the Body of Christ we can all prophesy, but some have been gifted to prophesy and some walk in the office of prophet. When we prophesy it should fall under three categories.

1 Corinthians 14:3 says, "But one who prophesies strengthens others, encourages them, and comforts them."

For a person who doesn't walk in the office of prophet, who occasionally prophesies, or those who walk in the gift of prophecy, your prophetic words should be words that strengthen, encourage, and comfort. There has been confusion at times, because those who have the gift of prophecy have been labeled a prophet. Just because someone can prophesy well does not make them a prophet. The office of prophet carries a governing authority that the gift of prophecy does not.

Unfortunately, many have been put in the prophetic office when they only carried the gift of prophecy. Those who carry the gift of prophecy can prophesy in detail and accuracy, but that doesn't mean they walk in a prophetic office. It's important to know what you walk in and stay in your lane. Leader it's important to distinguish those who truly walk in the office of prophet and those who have the gift of prophecy. Wrongly appointing or self appointing oneself to the prophetic office will bring unnecessary warfare, and could cause a causality of war because there is not a clear understanding of what a person walks in.

Word of Knowledge

A word of knowledge is when the Lord reveals information, or knowledge about a person or situation that was not previously known to the one releasing it. This can be a very powerful tool used in the prophetic. When a word of knowledge is given, it helps to build person's faith to receive a prophetic word. A word of knowledge is like a bridge connecting a person to the heart of God.

Before releasing a prophetic word, prepare the person's heart with a word of knowledge. A word of knowledge makes a person feel like God truly knows them and loves them. A word of knowledge makes a person feel as if they are seen by God. Many feel God is so distant and unreachable. Words of knowledge can penetrate even the hardest of hearts and those who doubt.

> *A word of knowledge is like a bridge connecting a person to the heart of God.*

Words of knowledge are often used to partner with healing. A word of knowledge can come through a pain in one's body that someone else is having. It can come through hearing the Lord, through a knowing, in dreams, or in a vision. The word of knowledge is a great tool to use when evangelizing. It releases the heart of the Father, and makes people feel known. With any gifting, word of knowledge also requires risk and stepping out in faith. Don't be discouraged if you miss it. There is grace to grow in accuracy.

Let's look at a couple examples of how the Bible portrays the word of knowledge. In 1 Samuel 9 we see the introduction of Saul who would be coming on the scene. Israel was asking for a King at this time because they wanted to be like other nations. Saul and his father's servant was out looking for his father's donkeys because they were lost. They went through a couple different towns but they couldn't find the donkeys. In verse 5 they have reached the district of Zupa and the servant in the next verse said, "Let's go see the man of God, he is highly respected, and everything he says is true. Let's go see the seer." (1 Samuel 9:6,9). Saul and his servant were about to walk into a divine encounter.

As the men began to approach the prophet, the Lord reminded the prophet that he revealed the day before a man from Benjamin would be coming, who would govern over the people of Israel (1Samuel 9:16, 17). As Saul meets Samuel, the prophet tells him you're going to dine and stay with me for the night, and by the way your donkeys are safe and have been captured. At the end of the chapter and into the next, Saul is getting ready to leave and anoints him as king (1 Samuel 10). Who knew getting a word about lost donkeys would turn into a divine setup? Words of knowledge lead to divine encounters.

Words of knowledge are attached to purpose. In Acts 9 we come across another Saul. Saul had an encounter with the Lord where he was knocked off his horse and blinded, and he was lead to Damascus where he stayed. In Damascus there was a disciple named Ananias, and the Lord brought him into a vision. The Lord called his name and told him to go to the house of Judas on Straight Street and ask for a man from Tarsus named Saul, for he is praying (Acts 9:10-11). Saul was praying and the Lord showed him a man would be coming to place his hands on Saul to restore His sight. As you go on throughout the chapter Ananias argues with the Lord because of all the things he heard about Saul.

One of the things about the revelatory and prophetic giftings is, you must love the person more than the gifting you walk in. Sometimes God will call you like Ananias to go to someone you may not like. A true prophet or prophetic person is not concerned whether they like a person. They release the word of the Lord because of love.

> *Words of knowledge are attached to purpose.*

Word of Wisdom

Many times, we get prophetic words or instruction and we don't know how to apply it or what to do in a matter. Words of wisdom give us strategy and understanding in how to apply and walk out what God is calling. When we release words of wisdom, we are releasing the counsel of God. His counsel is His thought process and His ways. Isaiah 55:8-9 declares, *"My thoughts are nothing like your thoughts, and My ways are far beyond anything you could imagine.*

For just as the heavens are higher than the earth so my ways are higher than your ways and my thoughts higher than your thoughts."

It says in the word that anyone who lacks wisdom should ask God who gives it out generously (James 1:5). Many times, we want word after word but we don't know how to fully inhabit it. Wisdom enables you to inhabit the word of the Lord. The wisdom of the Lord is needed to live in all He has for us. We are able to access the wisdom of God through the word and having the mind of Christ (1 Corinthians 2:16).

Not only do we need to access the mind of Christ, we need to access the council of God in the heavenly. When we are dealing with nations and governments and such, we need the council of God. This is the place where judgements and rulings are released. We can see references to His council throughout the Bible. His council is made up of Himself, other spiritual beings, and those who he appoints (Ps 89-5-8). In Jeremiah 23:18 it says, *"For who has stood in the council of the Lord to see and hear His word? Who has paid attention to His word and obeyed?"*

As prophets, standing in the council of God will be something of a common occurrence especially if you have a mantle for the nations. Moses in a great example of moving in and out of the council of God. The Lord taught Moses how to lead the Israelites. There were many times the Lord was ready to smite the Israelites, but Moses would go to God on their behalf. When God wanted to wipe out Sodom and Gomorrah, Abraham began to talk with God back and forth about saving the righteous even though the city was corrupt (Genesis 18). As prophets of God standing in the council of God is a normal occurrence.

The Spirit of Prophecy

When the spirit of prophecy hits a people or invades a service, it enables individuals to prophesy that would not normally prophesy. It's a heavenly realm that enters a place or a person, and they become a spokesman for the Lord in that moment. The spirit of prophecy is the testimony of Jesus (Revelation 19:10). The spirit of prophecy testifies and releases what heaven is saying in that moment.

If someone is not as inclined to the prophetic, when they get around prophets or prophetic people they can begin to prophesy or see because of what those prophetic people carry. It's always good to get around those who are further in the prophetic because it helps to bring you into a new place you've not been, in the prophetic.

We see an example of this in 1 Samuel 10 and 19 with Saul. In the beginning of chapter 10 the prophet Samuel told Saul he would run into a band of prophets and prophesy. 1 Samuel 10:10 says, *"When Saul and his servant arrived in Gibeah, they saw a group of prophets moving toward them. Then the Spirit of God came powerfully upon Saul, and he began to prophesy."* As this happened the people were amazed because like the prophets, Saul began to prophesy as if he was one of them.

> **Words of knowledge are attached to purpose.**

When the spirt of prophecy comes it enables you to prophesy and release what the Lord is saying.

We also see the spirit of prophecy being released in the New Testament in the upper room. In Acts 2 the disciples and the believers waited for the promise of the Holy Spirit to come. As they waited, the spirit of God came in like a mighty rushing wind and filled them all. They began to speak in different tongues as the Holy Spirit enabled them. As they went out to the streets the people around them began to hear their own native language.

When the spirit of prophecy comes upon us it transforms us and enables us prophesy from a heavenly realm.

Discerning of Spirits

Those who operate in discerning of spirits are able to discern the source and intention behind a matter or person. Hebrews 5:14 says, *"But solid food is for the mature, who because of practice have their senses trained to discern good and evil."* Discerning of spirits can be hard to navigate in the beginning of discovering this gift.

Many times people who operate in this gift don't realize they have it. When a person is discerning the matter or spirit behind something, their emotions or body may begin to be affected by the atmosphere they're in or the person next to them. Those who discern, often can tell who the bad egg is a room before others know.

There are three sources we discern from, the spirit of God, the demonic, and the flesh. When we operate in discernment God is giving us insight or showing us a secret about a person. To mature in this gifting, you have to learn to discern your emotions and what is going on around you. There have been times where I've woken up and have felt a heaviness for no reason. I had to ask the Lord if this is something going on in me, or am I picking up on something going on in the region. The Lord may also bring someone to mind or a feeling about something. Don't ignore it follow up with the person or ask the Lord how He wants you to pray through.

In the beginning of growing in this gifting a person can feel overwhelmed by all they are picking up on. Sometimes a person can pick up on so much, sensory overload can occur. When that happens, know there is grace to grow and mature and learn how to handle this gifting. We can discern through sensing, tactical feeling, hearing, smelling, tasting, a knowing. I remember being in a prayer meeting, as someone began to talk and pray my spirit got so agitated. The sound they were releasing was impure because of stuff going on in their heart. The sound in the spirit realm was like nails on a chalk board to me.

As you grow in this gifting it's important that you operate in love. If we're not careful discernment can grow into judgment, there is a fine line between them. This gift will allow you to see into people and discern hearts and motives good or bad. That's a powerful tool, because God is sharing secrets with you. One has to learn they cannot share everything the Lord shows them. There will be times you will have to confront a person because of what the Lord shows you, but often times the Lord reveals because He trust you to pray.

Discerning of spirits is a vital gift in this hour, and greatly needed in the Body of Christ because it reveals what's hidden. The Lord shows you the face behind the face. In operating in this gift it's important to not become suspicious of people, but it can protect you from toxic relationships or assignments the enemy might send to your church. In discerning there's been an emphasis on the demonic

> *To operate properly in this gifting our hearts have to stay in love.*

and negative. The Lord doesn't want us to just discern the negative. He desires for us to discern the godly and heavenly things. We have to make sure we find balance in this gifting and not lean more to one side or the other.

To operate properly in this gifting our hearts have to stay in love, and we must operate in love always (1 Corinthians 13). You have to learn to be able to handle what you discern, and God shows you about others and situations. Walking in love and humility is important to exercising this gift, because pride can taint your gifting. Also, find those who you can help process what your sensing and help you mature.

Dreams and Vision

Dreams and visions are part of the seer or seeing realm in the prophetic. Throughout the Bible there are many stories where the Lord would release dreams and visions for warnings, instruction, and encounters. I believe more than ever the Lord is releasing an increase of dreams and visions upon his people. Joel 2:28 says, *"Your old men will dream dreams, your young men will see visions."*

Dreams tend to be more symbolic and have their own language. Visions tend to be clearer and not as complicated to figure out what the Lord is saying. In Joel 2:28, the Bible says old men will dream dreams, that means they are more mature and able to figure out the symbolism. Young men is a reference to growing into maturity, so the Lord makes it more plain for those growing. Dreams and visions are an invitation to grow deeper in revelation and intimacy with the Lord.

Everyone has their own dream language the Lord speaks to them through. Dreams tend to be very symbolic, and the Lord will speak to you through symbols that you understand. We can also gain understanding in our dreams by looking up symbols in the Bible. Be careful of the resources you use to help with dream interpretation. Make sure you are using biblical and godly sources, because many dream interpretation sources are laced with new age and ungodly sources. Most importantly ask the Holy Spirit to help you interpret your dreams and visions.

Most of the time your dreams tend to be about you. Depending on the calling or mantle you carry, this will influence the way you dream. Because prophets carry a certain authority, their dreams can contain warnings and insights, for people, churches, regions, nations, and more. Be careful who you share your dreams with.

Not everyone can handle or understand how God speaks to you in dreams. Learn from the life of Joseph. He was a dreamer that got himself in trouble because, he shared a dream in the wrong timing and was not received.

When the Lord releases visions, visions carry a more literal interpretation and not as much symbolism. You can have a vision where your eyes are seeing a vision as if its right in front of you playing like scenes from a movie. You can also have inner visions where you are seeing a picture or different scenes in your mind's eye.

In Acts 18:9-10 is says, *"One night the Lord spoke to Paul in a supernatural vision and said, 'Don't ever be afraid. Speak the words that I give you and don't be intimidated for I am with you.'"* Dreams and visions are a common way the Lord speaks to His people. It's important to steward what the Lord reveals and shows you. Journal and write down your dreams and visions or record them so you can go back over them. As you become a good steward of what God reveals, He will increase your dreams and visions.

The Office of Prophet

The office of prophet is one of the five fold offices and giftings that the Lord released to the Church when He ascended. Ephesians 4:11-13 says, *"And he has appointed some with grace to be apostles, and some with grace to be prophets, and some with grace to be evangelists, and some with grace to be pastors, and some with grace to be teachers. And their calling is to nurture and prepare all the holy believers to do their own works of ministry, and as they do this they will enlarge and build up the body of Christ. These grace ministries will function until we all attain oneness in the faith, until we all experience the fullness of what it means to know the Son of God, and finally we become one perfect man with the full dimensions of spiritual maturity and fully developed in the abundance of Christ."*

The main purpose of the prophet is not just to prophesy. The purpose of the prophet is to train and equip the Body of Christ. The prophet helps mature believers, so they can minister effectively in their lives. The prophet helps the Body learn how to hear the voice of God.

The prophet, along with the apostle is a part of the foundation the Church is built upon (Ephesians 2:20). The prophet, along with the five-fold gifts operate in a governmental authority. The government of God and the laws of God supersede the natural. Prophets challenge corrupt and ungodly systems to establish the Kingdom of God. Every prophet has a realm of jurisdiction or authority they function in. You are most effective in the realm you are called to.

> ***Prophets carry the backing of Heaven.***

Prophets are ambassadors or representatives sent on behalf of the Kingdom of God. Anywhere the Kingdom is not manifested, the prophets help to establish it. Prophets are not meant to just reside in the church. We need prophets in every mountain of society ruling and reining, establishing the Kingdom of heaven.

Prophets release the judgements of God.

Prophets carry the backing of heaven. Prophets work heavily in the angelic realm. Angelic help and assistance is always at their disposal. Prophets walk in the miraculous. They walk in great power and demonstration to back up the word of the Lord they release and carry.

Let's see how prophets challenge systems. Part of the prophetic mandate is to overthrow demonic systems and establish pure Godly systems. We see this in the story of the prophet Samuel. Samuel was born into a corrupt prophetic system. In 1 Samuel 2, Eli the priest and his sons were corrupt, and they did not know the Lord. They did not properly follow the instructions for preparing the sacrifice. Eli's sons corrupted the temple by sleeping with the women who came to the temple. There was no vision or prophetic voice being released in that time.

Instead of correcting his sons, Eli turned a blind eye. Eli did not teach his sons the way of the Lord in order from them to take his Father's place. A true sign of a prophet is their ability to raise up others around them. When Samuel was born, he not only represented a prophetic promise fulfilled, but the hope and promise of a new and pure prophetic system that would rise. Samuel would raise up a new prophetic order, and a new prophetic company that would know the ways of the Lord. Prophets release the kingdom and government of God.

Activation

As a prophetic person and prophet it's important to activate and grow your gift. Get around others who are further along and that you can learn from. I have found that some of your greatest training ground is going out to the grocery store. Practice on people you come across throughout your day. As you begin to step out more your confidence will grow. If you miss it, don't get discouraged. Tell those you're practicing on you're learning how to hear God's voice. That can open the door to an unexpected conversation about the Lord.

There were times when I first started out, I would seem to miss it a lot. But then you finally get that one, that causes your faith and confidence to grow. One summer I was enrolled in a school of the supernatural my church was putting on. In this season I was really learning to grow and mature in my gift. We had been given homework for the week to practice the word of knowledge. That night after class I had to stop for gas on the way home. I was pumping the gas, I noticed the manager was outside taking inventory. The Lord told me to go pray for her. I told the Lord, "No I'm too tired it's been a long day, it's late. I don't even know what to say to her." I began to have an internal war with the Lord. I put the gas pump back, got back in my car and started the car. As I was getting ready to leave I heard the say, "Go pray for her, her daughter is sick. She has cancer." I thought "Oh great, she's going to think I'm crazy". I could no longer ignore the nudging of the Holy Spirt and the pit in my stomach. I approached her and introduced myself, I asked her if she had a daughter and if she was sick. You would have thought I was an alien the way she looked at me, her eyes were a big as saucers. She confirmed that she did indeed have a daughter that was in remission, but recently the cancer had returned. I was able to pray with her and let her know there was a God who loved her and her family, and He wanted to touch their lives. That encounter encouraged me and boosted my confidence to keep stepping out. People are waiting to know there is a God who knows them, loves them, and cares about what they're going through.

Your Prophetic Voice

AND HE GAVE SOME WITH THE GRACE TO BE PROPHETS...EPHESIANS 4:11

In the prophetic we have a crisis. There are too many prophets who sound the same and have become one dimensional. It's more than just prophesying about the blessings of God, the true prophetic also releases the hard words. There are too many prophets are trying to sound like one another, instead of learning to stand out and be the prophetic voice God has called them to be.

When you read throughout the Bible you can see there were no two prophets who were the same. Each prophet has their own prophetic signature and personality. Each prophetic voice releases a different facet of the prophetic. God wants to restore the fullness of the prophetic, and it starts with learning to be confident with the voice God has given you. It's ok to stick out. The thing that causes you to stick out is the prophetic edge the Lord has given you. Our prophetic edge becomes dull when we try to fit in or allow comparison to get into our hearts.

The Word of the Lord

As you begin to grow in your prophetic voice, it's important to know how the word of the Lord flows and operates. One of the main Hebrew words used for prophet in the Old Testament was *nabiy* or *nabi* Deuteronomy 18:18 says, *"I will raise up a prophet (nabiy) like you from among their fellow Israelites. I will put my words in his mouth, and he will tell the people everything I command him."* The word prophet in this verse is the nabi. The nabi function refers to how the prophet prophesies. As the prophet is unctioned to speak, the word of the Lord begins to bubble up or flow forth like a fountain. As prophets it's important to get in the word of God, so there is word in you the spirit can flow from. Nabi prophets tend to flow spontaneously as the hear the word of the Lord.

Next is the *nataf,* which means to drop like rain, a soaking, and saturation of the word. Deuteronomy 32:2 says, *"Let my teaching fall on you like rain; let my speech settle like dew. Let my words fall like rain on tender grass, like gentle showers on young plants"* Where the nabi function is more spontaneous, the nataf slowly builds up soaks and absorbs the word of the Lord. It carries a weightiness to it to open up atmospheres and realms.

Another way the word of the Lord makes come on an individual is the burden of the Lord. The Hebrew word massa refers to the burden of the Lord. Jeremiah 23:33 says, *"Suppose one of the people or one of the prophets or priests asks you, 'What prophecy has the* LORD *burdened (massa) you with now?' You must reply, 'You are the burden!*[a] *The* LORD *says he will abandon you!'* When the burden of the Lord comes upon a prophet, it weighs down the prophet in their spirit. They feel the weight or the heaviness of the word of God in them. The weight or the burden is not released from them until the prophet releases the word of the Lord. When it's released, it's like a weight lifted off the prophet. Sometimes prophets can seem serious, but it's because of the weight, burden, fear of the Lord they carry with the word God has placed on the inside of them.

The last way the Lord can impart the word of the Lord is through the seer or seeing realm. These prophets see the word of the Lord, whereas the nabi prophets hear the word of the Lord. The two Hebrew words for seer are *chozeh* and *ra'ah,* this deals more with the revelatory realm. Chozeh means a beholder in vision. Ra'ah means to see, to gaze, to look upon, and to perceive. One who operates in the seer realm must be sensitive to the spirit and submit their senses to the Lord.

Types of Prophets

Seers are prophets who hear the word of the Lord through seeing. All prophets have the ability to see in some measure. Seers perceive or discern the word through their senses and their spiritual vision. Seer prophets deal with heavy warfare because they are so sensitive to the spirit. The enemy will often to try to shut down their spiritual vision. An example of a seer prophet would be Jeremiah. In Jeremiah 1 the Lord began to teach Jeremiah how to see in the realm of the spirit and see the word of the Lord. It's important for seer prophets to be able to perceive what they are seeing and be able to articulate it to others.

Shamar or watchmen prophets are those who guard the spiritual gates over families, churches, regions, nations, and so on. They have the authority to govern what is allowed in those spiritual gates and what is not. Shamar is Hebrew for "to guard or protect". Often times these shamar prophets are intercessors. Not all intercessors are prophets, but all prophets are intercessors.

Shamar prophets are not ones to necessarily give prophetic words on a regular basis. They will mostly operate in prayer and will release words of warning to prepare the people of God. The warning is given to help protect and preserve the people. An example of a watchman prophet is Ezekiel. Shamar prophets sound the alarm. Ezekiel 33:7-9, *"Now, son of man, I am making you a watchman for the people of Israel. Therefore, listen to what I say and warn them for me. If I announce that some wicked people are sure to die and you fail to tell them to change their ways, then they will die in their sins, and I will hold you responsible for their deaths. But if you warn them to repent and they don't repent, they will die in their sins, but you will have saved yourself."* Shamar prophets are vital to the Body of Christ. They see the breaches and cracks in the spiritual walls the enemy tries to penetrate. They warn the Church of impending disasters and crisis to prepare and preserve the Body of Christ.

Dreamers are those who function in that seer realm, but primarily hear or see the word of the Lord through dreams. In the culture in the Bible it was very common for the Lord to speak to his people and different leaders through dreams. It was a way of personal encounter, and a way the Lord would speak to leaders and kings that would be prideful in their heart to listen.

Joseph the dreamer is found in Genesis 37. When he was young the Lord gave him a dream that he would one day rule over his brothers. He immaturely shared that with his brothers. His brothers got jealous and tried to kill him. Dreamers must be careful sharing dreams. Everyone is not able to handle what God shows.

It's important to discern when to share dreams. Later in Joseph's life the Lord gave him the opportunity to interpret Pharaoh's dreams. It enabled him to help save and preserve a nation. Hosea 12:13 says, *"The Lord used a prophet to bring Israel up from Egypt, by a prophet he was protected."*

Interpreters are those who have the gift to interpret dreams. I believe this is one area the Lord wants to strengthen in the Body. There are many who have dreams, but there is a lack of those who can interpret what God is speaking. We need godly people to go into different realms of society to interpret the dreams of leaders.

Another example of a dream interpreter was Daniel. Daniel was a prophet who God placed in leadership in a foreign government. King Nebuchadnezzar had a series of dreams and his astrologers could not interpret the dream, they suggested to get Daniel (Daniel 2). Daniel prayed and asked God to give him the interpretation of the dream. Daniel 2:22 says, *"He reveals deep and mysterious things and knows what lies in darkness."* Daniel was bold and told the king no wisemen or enchanters could reveal the king's secret but God. God used Daniel to do just that.

Governmental prophets are those God uses to enforce the government of God in many different spheres of society. Example of governmental prophets are Daniel and Joseph. Governmental prophets help preserve rulers and nations, using God's wisdom and counsel. Laws in put into place by God's wisdom. A prophet gives wisdom and insight in how God wants to rule, reign and be a part of a governmental system.

Minstrels and *Psalmists* are prophets who prophesy the word of the Lord through music, or by releasing the song of the Lord.
Both are a vital part of the Body of Christ. When the song of the Lord is sung, it releases the heart of the Father for that church or region. Minstrels prophesy on their instruments, by releasing different notes and chords that unlock different realms in the spirit and can subdue warfare. This is true of David. Saul would call upon him when he was feeling demonically oppressed. As David would play his hard the evil spirit would leave (1 Samuel 6:23).

Minstrels don't just play sounds, they open realms. Releasing the sound of heaven is just as important as releasing the song of the Lord. The sound of the Lord releases His power. 2 Kings 3:15 says, "Now bring me someone who can play the harp. While the harp was being played the power of the Lord came upon Elisha." Many times, churches stay stagnant because there is no prophetic worship. Prophetic worship allows a church and ministry to stay fresh, and step into new places in God each service. Prophetic worship was an important part of the Bible, and it should be for us. David raised up a whole company and generation of prophetic minstrels and psalmists. He taught them how to steward the presence of God in the temple, and the power of worship on the battlefield. David raised up a man named Asaph and his sons to play and lead them into battle (1 Chronicles 25:1-2).

We must put an emphasis in our churches to not just have great musicians and singer, but those who can prophetically release the sound and song of the Lord. The Lord wants to release fresh vision and prophetic realms for His Body to move forward. Churches stay stagnant and dry for lack of vision. Prophetic worship releases refreshing and fresh vision over a church.

Scribes are prophets who write the word of the Lord out. In the Bible especially the Old Testament, the prophetic scribes would write the word of the Lord on scrolls. These scrolls were delivered to who the Lord instructed. Scribes were those who wrote the books of the Bible.

In Habakkuk 2, the prophet Habakkuk talks about going to the watchtower to see what the Lord says and write it down. Habakkuk writes the vision to give to the herald, and the herald runs to release the word where they go. Ezra was another powerful example of a scribe. He was alive during a time where the people forgot the laws of God. They were no longer written on the heart of God's people, and it grieved him. Ezra began to call the people of God back to His standards.

Once again God is raising up scribes in this hour. He is raising up prophetic writers to influence different realms of society. Psalm 45:1 says, "My tongue is that of a ready writer." God wants to use His scribes to release His heart and write on the hearts of His people. God uses scribes to write the vision, so the Church doesn't forget the word of the Lord.

Issachar prophets are those who have an anointing to know the times and seasons. Ecclesiastes 3:1 says, *"There is a time and a season for every activity under the heavens."* I believe more than ever the Body of Christ needs those who carry the Issachar anointing. Many times we miss seasons individually and corporately because we miss the timing of the Lord. Issachar prophets help us maximize the timing and seasons of God.

The Issachar anointing comes from the tribe of Issachar. 1 Chronicles 12:32 says, *"From the tribe of Issachar were 200 leaders of the tribe. All these men understood the signs of the times and knew the best course for Israel to take."* God is raising up those who will be able to bring discernment and understanding to governments, churches, and other realms of society.

A Prophet's Lifestyle

JESUS OFTEN WITHDREW TO THE WILDERNESS TO PRAY LUKE 5:16

A prophet cannot live however they want. The prophetic call is a high call of surrender. The greater the realms and facets of the office you want to walk in, the greater the surrender and purity is required. A prophet must live a consecrated set apart life. Prophets must guard purity at all costs. If the vessel is tainted so will the prophetic coming from them.

Jesus was our greatest example as a prophet. He lived a life of consecration and prayer. Jesus would often sneak away to a hidden place to pray and hear from the Father. Prophets, we never outgrow the place of prayer. Prayer is our power source and place of revelation. A prophet is marked by their prayer life. There are a lot of prophets that hang around the presence of God, but never prophesy from the presence of the Lord. We see this in the story of Eli and his sons in 1 Samuel 3. They were put in charge of the sacrifices and stewarding the presence of God. They became so common with God's presence they lacked reverence for protecting and defiled it. Prophets are protectors of the presence and word of God.

Prophet don't let your heart be for sale for money or popularity. As you start out on this journey set in your heart this day for no compromise. Any door we leave open gives the enemy an opportunity to tempt us. When you prostitute your gift, you become a puppet instead of a prophet.

> *Prophets never outgrow the place of prayer.*

Don't Look Behind

One of the greatest examples of someone who truly lived out the prophetic lifestyle was Elisha. Elisha served his way to gaining his prophetic mantle. Many prematurely expect a mantle to just fall on them. To inhabit your mantle, you must pursue it at all costs. Mantles are not just given, they're caught.

Each prophet will have their "Elijah" that will call them forth and out. In 1 Kings 19, Elijah found Elisha plowing the fields when Elijah called upon him. Every prophet has to make the choice to accept it all. Just as Jesus called forth the disciples to lay down their lives and follow him, we must do that as prophets. Don't leave any escape routes back to your former lives. Many prophets leave open doors that don't allow them to fully function in their call.

After Elisha becomes Elijah's servant there is not much mentioned of him till 2 Kings. God will bring prophets through hidden seasons to prepare them for their visible seasons. God will often put us under someone to see if we are humble and willing to serve another man's vision or ministry, before God will give you your ministry. There's a blessing that's released when we can serve others. Sowing isn't just about money, we sow our time and who we are.

As Elisha served Elijah, he was also a part of a school of prophets. Schools of prophets have the ability to separate potential, and those who will answer the call. Before Elijah was taken to heaven, he tested Elisha before Elisha received the mantle. God allows the testing to prepare us for the mantle.

The band of prophets with Elijah began to give Elisha a hard time. They asked him, *"Did you know that the Lord was going to take your master away today? Yes of course I know, be quiet, answered Elisha" (2 Kings 2:3-4).* It's important to guard against jealousy and competition. The other prophets weren't willing to do what it took to catch the mantle, Elisha did. I believe they all could've gotten a portion of the mantle. The other prophets weren't willing to serve and pursue after Elijah's mantle. The mantle will cost you something to inhabit it.

Prophets are deliverers.

Warfare

A prophetic lifestyle will include dealing with warfare on a regular basis. In Ephesians 6:12 it says, *"We are not fighting against flesh and blood enemies, but against evil rulers and authorities of*

the unseen world, and against evil spirits in heavenly places."
Prophets are called to dismantle principalities and ungodly systems of government that try to exalt themselves above the Lord.

Prophets and prophetic people are a threat to the Kingdom of darkness. A part of the mantle is to confront darkness and spirits holding nations, regions, families, and the people of God in bondage. Prophets are deliverers. Prophets and Apostles deal with warfare more than most because they are pioneers that lead and break open the way for the Kingdom of God to manifest. There are certain spirits that target the prophetic.

The Jezebel Spirit

The *Jezebel spirit* is a spirit of assassination against the prophetic spirit and prophets. Jezebel hates the prophetic and will do everything in its power to kill the prophetic. The Jezebel spirit is mentioned in Revelation 2:20, *"But I have this complaint against you. You are permitting that woman that Jezebel who calls herself a prophet to lead my servants astray. She teaches them to commit sexual sin and to eat food offered to idols."* 1 Kings 16:31 describes Jezebel, *"Ahab married Jezebel, the daughter, of King Ethebaal of the Sidionians, and he began to bow down in worship of Baal.*

The spirit of Jezebel is a seducing spirit that leads people into sexual sin and idolatry. As soon as Jezebel married Ahab, he built a temple and an altar for Baal in Samaria. He also put up an Asherah pole to provoke the anger of the Lord (1 Kings 16:32-33). Baal is known as a fertility god worshiped in the east, especially by the Canaanites (Britannica.com). He was also known as Lord of the rain and the lord of the heavens. Throughout the land Asherah poles were erected displaying sexual images throughout the land.

The Jezebel spirit breaks covenant. The Jezebel spirit always has an agenda. She caused the Israelites to break covenant with God, and worship other gods and defile the land. The Jezebel spirit has an agenda to overthrow and impose its kingdom. This spirit is no respecter of gender. A male or female can operate in the Jezebel Spirit.

The Jezebel spirit is not just a spirit, it's a ruling reigning principality. The Jezebel gains access through unhealed wounds and traumas. Principalities influence people's thought processes through open spiritual doors. The Jezebel spirit is crafty. It uses flattery, manipulation, control, fear to get its way. Jezebel will stroke your ego as long as you go with it.

The Jezebel spirit is a false prophetic spirit. This spirit can prophesy, but it operates from a power source that is not the Lord. Jezebel will often attack the prophetic and prayer areas of a church, to try and establish its throne in the spirit. Jezebel wants to cut off the head of the prophetic spirit. We see examples of this with the prophet Elijah and John the Baptist. In 1 Kings 19 after the showdown with Jezebel's prophets, Elijah slayed them. Jezebel sent a messenger to tell Elijah she was going find him and kill him. This message was laced with fear and it gripped Elijah's heart. It paralyzed him for a time until God set him free and he helped to finish Jezebel off.

> *The Jezebel spirit always has an agenda.*

In Matthew 14, Herodias's daughter performed a dance for Herod that greatly pleased him. Because Herod was pleased, he told her he would give her anything she wanted. At the mother's urging the daughter requested the head of John the Baptist on a tray. Herod granted the wish of the daughter. Jezebel wants to cut the prophetic off at all cost.

The Jezebel spirit will be upon the earth until the Lord judges and deals with it in the end. Just because the Jezebel spirit is upon the earth doesn't mean it needs to be tolerated. We get in trouble when we allow Jezebel to reign in our lives, churches, and regions. Where the Jezebel spirit is, there will be idolatry and impurity.

As a prophet and prophetic person, you will face different levels of this spirit Jezebel. The level of severity will depend on the maturity of the Jezebel spirit in the person. The Jezebel spirit takes over the mind and becomes a mindset. This spirit preys upon the wounded and will flatter to get others to do its bidding. Refuse to eat and sit at Jezebel's table it will lead to spiritual death.

In my experience, when getting hit with Jezebel witchcraft, you may feel like you want to pull the covers over your head and stay in bed. You feel a loss of energy, headaches, dizziness, migraines. This witchcraft is released to push you back and keep you in the cave like it did Elijah. Like Elijah you will tend to feel alone and isolated. Reach out to others for prayer, and don't allow the Jezebel spirit to silence your prophetic voice.

The Python Spirit

The ***python or spirit of divination*** is another spirit a prophet will deal with. Like the spirit of Jezebel this spirit can work through an individual or can be a ruling principality. The intent of the python spirit is to choke the life out of the individual or a region.

The prophetic spirit is a life-giving spirit. When the prophetic spirit is released, the *ruach*, or the breath of God is released upon an individual and region. Where the python spirit is there is a hopelessness, passion is lost, there is weariness, heaviness, and this spirit chokes the vison and purpose out. The python spirit will attack your prayer life, because your prayer life is your life line to the spirit of God. We see this example in Acts 16, as Paul and Silas were on the way to prayer they encountered a girl who had a spirit of divination. This girl followed them around say things that were true, "These men are servants of the Most High God, and they have come to tell you how to be saved" (Acts 16:17). She was right in what she was saying, but the source of the information was coming from an ungodly source…divination. Paul became irritated in his spirit because, the girl was operating in a demonic spirit and was mocking them. Paul called it out and the girl was delivered. By Paul casting out this spirit it was being overthrown in the region. The girl's masters were not happy because they were earning money off of her false words.

    Those who operate in divination operate in a false prophetic spirit, or strange fire. They are getting their prophetic words and revelation from familiar spirits. Those operating in the python spirit can be hard to discern because it can prophesy to a point. The python spirit can operate or gain access through those who are wounded or those seeking the supernatural, and not accessing the spirit realm through the Lord.

    We live in a society that is hungry for the supernatural. There are many operating in divination thinking they are operating in the spirit of God. In the prophetic it's important to be grounded in the word of God and be in relationship with the Father. It's imperative to test the spirits around and the supernatural experiences you have.

To avoid operating in divination, it's important to stay close to the refining fire. When we allow God to refine us it gives the enemy less access into our lives. When you stay close to the fire of God you're able to spot a false spirit. In Acts 28, Paul was sitting next to the fire when a snake bit him. He was able to shake the snake off into the fire.

Those in divination tend to tap into different sources of magic, witchcraft, sorcery, etc. Divination uses witchcraft to cause things to happen or release prophetic words that are false. There is usually a motive behind the divination being released.

> *Those who operate in divination operate in a false prophetic spirit.*

Deuteronomy 18:10-12 says, "Let no one be found among you who sacrifices their son or daughter in the fire, who *practices divination or sorcery interprets omens, engages in witchcraft, or casts spells, or who is a medium or spiritist, or who consults the dead. Anyone who does these things is detestable to the Lord."* The true prophetic spirit will always point back to Jesus and release the heart of the Father.

The Religious Spirit

One of the main oppositional spirits to the prophetic and revival, is the religious spirit. The religious spirit is rooted in tradition and rituals. This spirit will try to assassinate the prophetic spirit. The religious spirit uses the law and works to keep the people bound.

This spirit will say, "This is how we have always done things. The religious spirit doesn't like when the prophetic comes and disrupts what has always been done. The religious have a system in which keeps the people of God bound. It's a form of control and manipulation.

Religion says that you're not justified by faith, but that you have to follow and keep the rules and regulations to be made right. Religion is grounded in legalism. Romans 5:1 says, *"Therefore, since we have been justified by faith, we have peace with God through our Lord Jesus Christ."* The spirit of religion makes someone, or a church look good on the outside, but the inside carries not life. Jesus would often confront the religious and their tradition. The religious hold the people of God hostage.

The religious spirit knows the word and the things of God, but there is no revelation of His spirit. In the time of Jesus, the very one the religious read about, studied about and was looking for, they missed. They missed him because he didn't come in a way they thought he would.

The spirit of religion keeps the people dependent on the church, instead of upon the Lord. They keep the people bound through guilt, shame, and condemnation. The people are enslaved in the spirit and are never able to fully grow and mature. This spirit is afraid of others surpassing them.

The religious scholars always questioned Jesus about his identity, and where his authority came from. They believed their authority derived from their ability to know the scriptures and obey the religious laws. The religious make an idol out of their self-righteousness, but the Lord is nowhere in it. The religious spirit leaves no room for the Kingdom agenda.

The spirit of religion will deceive you and get you enslaved to the performance trap. It's like a hamster that runs on a wheel in its cage. It constantly spins in circles going nowhere. The religious will crucify what they don't understand. The religious have no radar for the prophetic spirit or kingdom agenda. It's all about building their kingdom, and keeping the people enslaved to rules and rituals.

When the prophetic spirit begins to confront religion, expect persecution and backlash. Don't allow its intimidations to stop you. It can be like walking into a hornet's nest. The spirit of religion is a form of godliness, but it lacks the power and demonstration of God. God desires for His church to free from religion and living in the freedom he died for on the cross.

Pitfalls

HOW CAN YOU TURN THE HEARTS OF MEN TO THE FATHER IF YOUR OWN HEART IS NOT FULLY TURNED TOWARDS HIM?- JENNIFER LECLAIRE

With anything in life especially in the prophetic, balance is key and essential. Balance and the guidelines the Lord has set within his word are safeguards to protect you from going too far to the left or right. Imagine spiritual bumpers like the bumpers children use at the bowling alley. The "prophetic ball" may not always go straight down the lane, but the bumpers are there so it doesn't fall in the gutter or pit.

What is a pitfall? A pitfall can be defined as a hidden, camouflaged, unsuspected danger, trap, or snare used to capture (merriam-webster.com). The enemy is very sneaky and strategic, and always looking for a way to cause you to slip or get stuck. He desires to make you ineffective or use you as a tool in his kingdom.

This chapter doesn't encompass all the pitfalls but will give you an awareness of some of the common ones an individual may experience at some point. It's beneficial to be aware and discerning of the tactics that will hinder your walk and flow in the prophetic.

****A half surrendered heart-*** To truly walk effectively in the prophetic, you must have a fully surrendered heart. When you answer the prophetic call, you are no longer yours, but your life has been given over to the Lord to be His mouth piece. If our hearts are halfway surrendered, it will open the door to error. Halfway surrendered hearts become a playground for the enemy, enabling him to persuade your heart in the wrong way. Hearts that are not fully surrendered can be easily bought. To be effective and have longevity the Lord must have your whole heart.

****Lack of Accountability*** -There's a dangerous trend in the prophetic, where prophets and prophetic people believe accountability and being submitted under authority is a bad thing.

Accountability brings safety and protection. Jesus sent the disciples out in twos. In the Body of Christ, we must break out of the lone ranger mentality, and embrace accountability. If a prophet or prophetic person cannot submit and have accountability, they have no business being in ministry or in the pulpit.

In the age of social media individuals self-appoint and give themselves an office they've not been processed for. Accountability helps keep prophets from error. It helps them to grow and stay balanced. 1 Corinthians 14:32 says, *"The spirts of the prophets are subject to the prophets."* Accountability is a safeguard.

Greater accountability is needed in prophesying words and keeping a track record. When we spit out prophetic words like its nothing, we lack a reverence for the office and the Lord. People are getting hurt and jaded, because prophets are prophesying things the Lord never said. Prophets must remember they have a great responsibility, because they are speaking the Lord's heart, mind, and will. Accountability keeps you grounded, keeps you from error, and it will allow your gift to mature and grow.

Not planted in the house of the Lord- This falls in line with accountability. Prophets belong in the house of the Lord. Just because one is a prophet doesn't exempt them from being a part of a church. The church is the bride of Christ to which prophets are called to. Psalm 92:13 says, *"Those planted in the house of the Lord they will flourish in the courts of God."* Some prophets are not flourishing because they're not planted in the house of the Lord. Yes, at times churches may misunderstand you and mistake you, but there is purpose in being in the house of the Lord. Prophets must fight the urge to isolate, and feel they are above the local assembly.

> *Accountability is a safeguard.*

****A lack of knowledge of the Word of God-*** A prophet prophesies from the foundation of the Word of God. It's important for prophets to be students of the word. The more word you know, the more you can pull from it. You prophesy from the word of God in you. Many are prophesying one dimensional word because their foundation of the word is shallow. Prophetic words never take the place of the word of God, they complement the word. The Lord will prophesy through you out of the knowledge you have of Him. The word of God is an anchor that helps to test the spirits around us and keep us from the things not of the Lord.

Don't stay stuck in warfare- As a prophet and prophetic person it's important to not get stuck and grounded in warfare. The prophetic mantle has the tendency to stir up and confront things in the spirit. We must discern when to engage and when to rest. The devil will wear us out. Prophets are called to be like the eagles, to soar above the second heaven warfare, and learn to function from the third heaven mentality.

Prophets must properly discern if the warfare is coming from outside of them, or from within them. Sometimes, prophets can be their own worst enemy. When there are open doors or places that need healing in our lives, it will attract warfare. It's important to learn when to engage in warfare and when to tune it out.

Don't try to make your spouse or those close to you like you- As prophetic people we love to have those around us that are similar. Prophets feed off of each other and can prophesy all day.

It's good to have other prophetic people around, but its also good to have those that are not necessarily prophetic around. Having others around us that are not like us brings balance.

Prophetic people tend to have their head in the clouds so to speak. We need those around us, especially our spouses to keep us grounded. In marriage there's a learning curve and adjustment when one spouse has a prophetic calling and the other may not function in the same capacity. Sometimes as spouses we can try to make the person like us, which will create a tension and strain in your marriage.

When considering marriage if you or your future spouse has a prophetic call, its important to consider the cost. Make sure there is an understanding of what that may look like. Personally, in the beginning of my marriage I knew I was a prophetic person but did not realize I was a prophet and all that it entailed until further along in our marriage. My husband and I are complete opposites.

It's humorous how different we are, but God knew what He was doing when He put us together. There was a time I did try to make my spouse more like me. As you can imagine that didn't go so

well. It took us a while, but we found our groove, and gave each other space to be who God created one another to be. My husband is my rock. He is very stable, calm, logical, has different gifts than me, and sees differently. These are a great compliment to a prophetic person who can be the complete opposite. Give your spouse the room to grow and be who it is that
God has made them to be, not who you want them to be. The Father knows what you need, trust Him.

Don't neglect soul care- I have found that every level or new place the Lord brings you to, another level of deliverance will be required. The higher you go in the realm of the spirit; the more purity is needed to access those places. There will be seasons where prophets will go through tremendous rejection and need healing. When we don't do soul care, we risk tainting the prophetic flow in our lives. If we're not careful we'll begin to project onto others what is our issues.

I want to encourage you to seek inner healing and deliverance. Sometimes deliverance comes in an instant, sometimes it's a process. There are times where I've had to pray through things with others. And there have been times where the Lord has brought deliverance to me through a dream. For a prophet to stay pure, deliverance and soul care must be a way of life.

Don't copy others be an original- One of the hardest things in the prophetic can be to find your voice. Prophets are similar, but each prophet carries a different voice. Resist the temptation to mimic yourself off of another person's ministry. You are the most anointed when you are yourself. Every prophet flows differently, whether that means loud, quiet, bold, meek, worship, painting, etc.

A prophet loses their prophetic edge when they try to fit in to be like the voices around them. It's about becoming comfortable in who God made you, and how He created you to function as a prophet. No one can prophesy and declare the word of the Lord like you can.

Don't allow discernment to turn into judgement- As prophets and prophetic people we must keep our discernment our discernment. The Lord doesn't allow us to discern or reveal things, for us to use it against others. Discernment reveals and uncovers secrets the Lord entrusts us with. Those secrets can be about a person, a church, a region, or other things. Those who discern often see the "snake" first.

Discernment is a powerful gift that can quickly turn into judgement when not done in love. Love should be the foundation and the basis for all that we do (1 Corinthians 13). To operate successfully in discernment, humility is required. Humility keeps our heart in the right posture. Because discernment reveals secrets, we have to guard our hearts from pride. Just because the Lord reveals secrets to you, doesn't make you better than those around. God shares His secrets with those He trusts, and those who can handle what is made known.

It's important to have balance in discerning. We have been really good at discerning the demonic and the negative. The Spirit of God did not give us discernment to just focus on the demonic. The Lord wants us to be able to discern His spirit, where He is working, and angelic assistance. Work on learning to discern both to remain in a healthy place. We will discern out of the lenses we wear.

Don't forsake the secret place- Prophets never forsake the secret place. There will be times when the Lord will bring you forth, and there will be times where He has us hidden. Remember our first mandate is stand before the Lord and in His council, not before man. There are too many prophets in this hour standing before man, and have forsaken the secret place.

Prophets carry and release the heart, mind, and will of the Father. To do that properly, one must spend time in the presence of God. The presence of God is where council, insight, revelation, and prophetic words are released. If a prophet lacks time in the presence of God, they can start releasing things from the soulish realm.

Don't forget to have fun- Sometimes being a prophet can get heavy. If you're not careful the weight of the calling can crush you. Prophets can be serious and need time to have fun. I want to encourage you to find a hobby or something that is outside of the prophetic. Prophets tend to be a loner. Do something that encourages you to be around others. Learn to laugh, and not take yourself so seriously. The Lord doesn't want you to be so serious that you forget to enjoy life and have fun. Having fun and learning to laugh, brings balance to a calling that can be very heavy at times.

PRAYER OF IMPARTATION

Father I pray those who have read this book will receive a fresh impartation of your Spirit. Breathe upon their spirit man and the prophetic giftings that reside within them. I pray a fresh fire and anointing upon them. May the word of the Lord be like a fire shut up in their bones. Give them the grace to endure the prophetic process that refine their gifts and character. I pray for the spirit of accuracy to be released over their gifts. I prophesy they will see in greater depths, dimensions, and with keen spiritual sight like never before. Give them ears to hear what the Spirit is saying, and boldness to release the word of the Lord wherever you send them. In Jesus' name amen.

ABOUT THE AUTHOR

Madeline James is an emerging prophetic voice who resides in Lexington, KY, with her husband and two beautiful girls. Madeline is the lead pastor of Ignite Winchester in Winchester, KY under Apostle Johnathan Stidham. She is the author of *Declaring Your Morning*, *Rooted In Love*, and co-author of *Emerge*. Madeline is the blogger of the prophetic blog Nabi's Pen. She desires to be a prophetic voice that propels and pushes the Body of Christ forward. Her website is nabispen.com

REFERENCES

Ferguson, Jonothan, (2013). *Prophets:101*

Leclaire, Jennifer, (2007). *The Heart Of The Prophetic*

YouVersionBible App-AMP, NLT, TPT

Made in the USA
Middletown, DE
12 March 2021